Sand to Glass

by Bryan Langdo

Blastoff! Readers are carefully developed by literacy experts to build reading stamina and move students toward fluency by combining standards-based content with developmentally appropriate text.

Level 1 provides the most support through repetition of high-frequency words, light text, predictable sentence patterns, and strong visual support.

Level 2 offers early readers a bit more challenge through varied sentences, increased text load, and text-supportive special features.

Level 3 advances early-fluent readers toward fluency through increased text load, less reliance on photos, advancing concepts, longer sentences, and more complex special features.

★ **Blastoff! Universe**

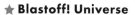

Reading Level

Grade **K**

Grades **1-3**

Grade **4**

This edition first published in 2024 by Bellwether Media, Inc.

No part of this publication may be reproduced in whole or in part without written permission of the publisher. For information regarding permission, write to Bellwether Media, Inc., Attention: Permissions Department, 6012 Blue Circle Drive, Minnetonka, MN 55343.

Library of Congress Cataloging-in-Publication Data

Names: Langdo, Bryan, author.
Title: Sand to glass / by Bryan Langdo.
Description: Minneapolis, MN : Bellwether Media, Inc., 2024. | Series: Blastoff! Readers. Beginning to end | Includes bibliographical references and index. | Audience: Ages 5-8 | Audience: Grades 2-3 | Summary: "Relevant images match informative text in this introduction to how sand is made into glass. Intended for students in kindergarten through third grade"– Provided by publisher.
Identifiers: LCCN 2023006493 (print) | LCCN 2023006494 (ebook) | ISBN 9798886874259 (library binding) | ISBN 9798886875355 (paperback) | ISBN 9798886876130 (ebook)
Subjects: LCSH: Glass–Juvenile literature. | Glass manufacture–Juvenile literature. | Sand–Juvenile literature.
Classification: LCC TP857.3 .L35 2024 (print) | LCC TP857.3 (ebook) | DDC 666/.1–dc23/eng/20230302
LC record available at https://lccn.loc.gov/2023006493
LC ebook record available at https://lccn.loc.gov/2023006494

Editor: Elizabeth Neuenfeldt   Designer: Laura Sowers

Printed in the United States of America, North Mankato, MN.

Table of Contents

Sand Becomes Glass

Do you know how glass is made?
It starts with sand!

Where Is Glass Made?

The United States makes over 12 million tons (10 million metric tons) of glass each year

A special **process** turns it into glass.

Under the Water

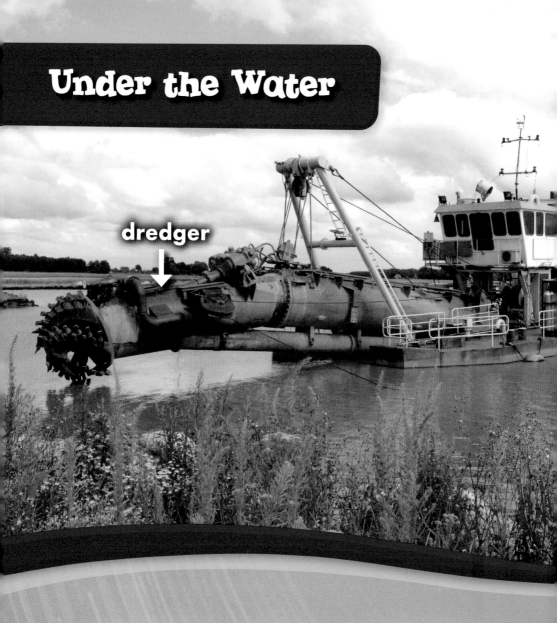

dredger

Sand comes from sand **mines**.
Sand mines are in oceans,
lakes, or rivers.

Using Sand

The world uses 55 billion tons (50 billion metric tons) of sand each year!

A **dredger** sucks up sand. The sand is poured into trucks.

Trucks bring the sand
to a glass factory.
The sand is mixed
with **soda ash**
and **limestone**.

It is also mixed with
recycled glass.

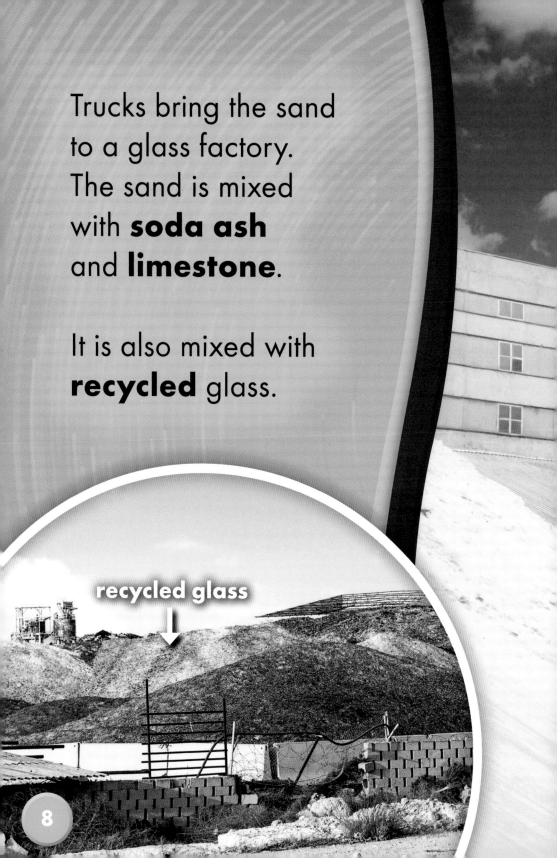

recycled glass

Bottles and Jars

10 out of 10 glass bottles and jars can be recycled

glass factory

Molten Glass

furnace

The sand mixture goes into
a **furnace**. It gets very hot.
Then it melts.

Molten glass comes out
of the furnace.

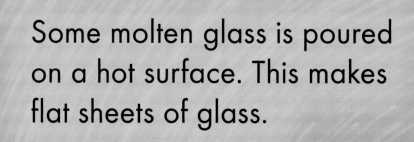

Some molten glass is poured on a hot surface. This makes flat sheets of glass.

sheets of glass

These sheets of glass will later become windows!

Some molten glass is cut into **gobs**. The gobs are poured into **molds**.

The molds shape gobs into jars or bottles.

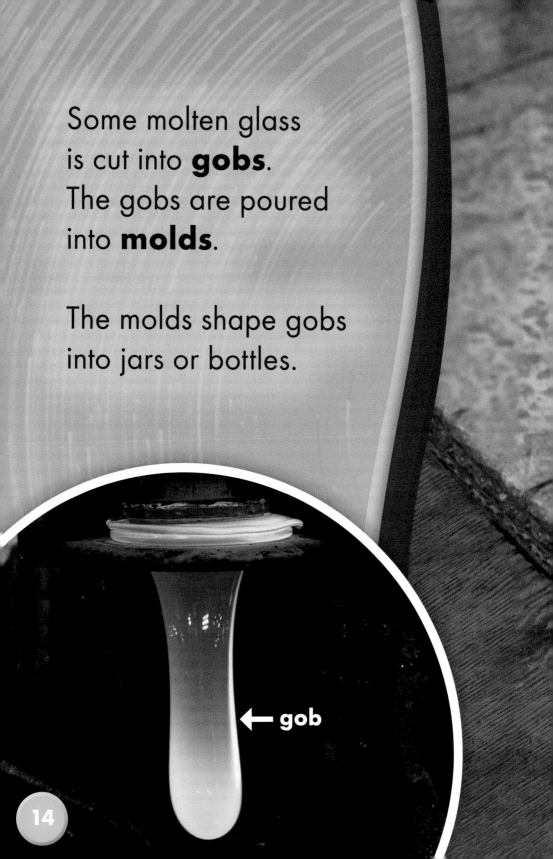

← gob

← **mold**

Parts of the Process

furnace

molds

Glassblowers also use gobs.
They grab the gobs with
a special pipe.

pipe

They blow into the pipe.
This helps glassblowers
make different shapes!

annealing glass

The hot glass is in the right shape.
It is ready to cool down!
The glass is **annealed**.
This keeps it from breaking.

Sand to Glass

1 sand is dredged from underwater

2 trucks bring the sand to a factory

3 the sand is mixed with other materials

4 the mixture is melted to make molten glass

5 molten glass is cut or poured into shape

6 the glass is annealed

Glass Is Everywhere

Many things are made of glass. Windows and phone screens have glass. Light bulbs are made of glass, too.

Glass is all around us!

Glossary

annealed—cooled down slowly so it will not break

dredger—a boat or machine that digs up sand from underwater

furnace—a structure that produces heat

glassblowers—people who make things out of glass

gobs—small pieces of molten glass

limestone—a type of rock used to build things and make glass

mines—places where people get materials like rocks, metal, or sand

molds—open containers in which substances can be shaped

molten—a liquid state from being heated

process—a number of steps taken to reach an end result

recycled—something that has passed through a series of processes so a material can be used again

soda ash—a powder used to make glass

To Learn More

AT THE LIBRARY

Houts, Michelle. *Sea Glass Summer*. Somerville, Mass.: Candlewick Press, 2019.

Rathburn, Betsy. *Glass Jar Crafts*. Minneapolis, Minn.: Bellwether Media, 2022.

Toolen, Avery. *From Sand to Glass*. Minneapolis, Minn.: Bullfrog Books, 2022.

ON THE WEB

FACTSURFER

Factsurfer.com gives you a safe, fun way to find more information.

1. Go to www.factsurfer.com.

2. Enter "sand to glass" into the search box and click 🔍.

3. Select your book cover to see a list of related web sites.

Index

The images in this book are reproduced through the courtesy of: Istvan Csak, front cover; a9photo, front cover; Saijai13, front cover (inset); Nimit Ketkham, p. 3; Ingrid Maasik, pp. 4-5; FOTO STEENHUIS, pp. 6-7; Sarit Richerson/ Alamy, pp. 8, 19 (3); croftsphoto/ Alamy, pp. 8-9; Traimak Ivan, pp. 10-11; Susan Sheldon, p. 11; Maksim Bogodvid/ AP Images, pp. 12-13; Akimov Igor, p. 13; Iceskatinggrizzly, p. 14; rdonar, pp. 14-15; Paul Cowan, p. 15 (furnace); Kodibeverlin, p. 15 (molds); Benoit Daoust, pp. 16-17, 19 (5); Florin Cnejevici, p. 17; Leslie Garland Pictures/ Alamy, p. 18; Heng Sinith/ AP Images, p. 19 (1); Place-to-be, p. 19 (2); Sonate, p. 19 (4); SviatlanaLaza, p. 19 (6); fizkes, pp. 20-21; encrier, p. 21; Nagel Photography, p. 23.